℗ CHILDRENS PRESS

OPEN DOOR

ABOUT THE COLLECTION: These auto... ...ns are relevant to youth today. Each person tells his life story just the way it happened, his ambitions, his struggle to a successful career. The books conclude with career guidance sections which detail the occupation of the author.

NEW: CALL IT FATE by William McCalip, black man and former addict, director of Illinois drug abuse program

NEW: CURSE NOT THE DARKNESS by Edison Hoard, a black lawyer

NEW: DON'T STOP ME NOW by Dempsey Travis, a black real estate executive

NEW: HEY, TAXI! by Adolphus Washington, a black cab driver

NEW: IRON MAN by Billy Williams, a black professional baseball player

NEW: MISSION POSSIBLE by Zenolia Leak, a black woman, teacher of airline reservation trainees

NEW: MY TRIBE by Joseph Vasquez, an American-Indian purchasing agent

NEW: NOBODY PROMISED ME by John Mack, Chairman of Black Studies, Chicago State College

NEW: ON MY OWN by Charles Davis, a black man prominent in the field of public relations

NEW: PEOPLE ARE MY PROFESSION by Herb Hannahs, a black public aid caseworker

NEW: RUN FOR YOUR LIFE by James Ellis, a black community social worker

NEW: UP FROM EL PASO by Paul Diaz, a Mexican-American building inspector

NEW: WEST SIDE COP by William Sims, a black police cadet

OTHER OPEN DOOR BOOKS:

A FOOT IN TWO WORLDS
EL RANCHO DE MUCHACHOS
GREAT SPIRIT
I REACHED FOR THE SKY
IN THE FACE OF THE SUN
MEIGS TOWER

NEW FIELDS
SOMEDAY I'M GOING TO BE SOMEBODY
WHATEVER YOU CAN'T HAVE
WHERE THERE'S SMOKE
WRITTEN ON FILM
YOU'RE ON THE AIR

SPECIFICATIONS:

illustrated with photos
64 pages/12 point type

reading level 5
for use with 7 & up

Library Edition

Childrens Press price
to Individuals
$3.00

Childrens Press price
to Schools and Libraries
$2.25

Paperback Edition
75¢

1224 West Van Buren Street, Chicago, Illinois 60607

WEST SIDE COP

OPEN DOOR BOOKS

WEST SIDE COP

By William Sims

With G. C. Skipper

Cover photos and photos on pages 2, 6, 48, 51, 53, 54, 55, and 56 by Jerry Jess.

Joan Downing: Project Editor

Margrit Fiddle: Art Director

Published by Childrens Press, Chicago, Illinois

Library of Congress Catalog Card Number 76-110038

1 2 3 4 5 6 7 8 9 10 11 12 13 14 15 16 17 18 19 20 21 22 23 24 25 R 75 74 73 72 71 70

CONTENTS

I SEE MYSELF

I was tense when I stepped out of the squad car and onto the dark sidewalk.

"Watch yourself, Bill," my partner said.

I looked back and smiled at him. He was sitting behind the wheel of the car and in the darkness I could see only the checkerboard pattern on the front of his cap.

"I grew up on these streets, remember?"

"Yeah, but he could be armed."

I closed the car door silently and walked toward the storefront at the end of the street. A lamp burned on the corner, just beyond the store. The Chicago night smelled damp and cold.

I had not gone more than ten steps when the door of the store burst open and a teen-ager ran out holding something under his arm.

"Hold it!" I shouted.

The sound of my own voice was startling and loud in the darkness. The boy stopped cold in his tracks. I dropped

Patrolman Richard Iwanowski is behind the wheel of the squad car we are cruising in.

down on one knee and pretended that I had a pistol in my right hand.

"Stop there and you won't get hurt," I told him.

The boy did as he was told and as I cautiously stood up, I heard the motor of the squad car crank over. My partner inched the car up the street. He brought it to a stop in front of the boy who stood on the sidewalk outside the store.

"Real slow now, fella," I said. "Let me see what you got there."

The boy handed a box to me. Inside was a radio. It was a small radio, and could not be very expensive. When I looked at it closer I realized it might even be secondhand. That boy got himself into a mess of trouble for a cheap radio, I thought.

My partner leaned the boy over the car and searched him.

"He's clean," my partner said.

"All right. Get in the car," I told the boy. "You're under arrest."

The squad car door swung open and the boy crawled inside.

I climbed into the car saying, "Let's go."

My partner hit the accelerator and we drove to the Eleventh District station.

"You stole a radio," I said. "What'd you want to go and do that for?"

"Quit preaching!"

My partner glanced at me across the front seat of the car. We both carefully kept our expressions blank. "You don't have to say anything, you know," my partner told me.

"Honky!" the boy said to him.

"Easy, kid," I said.

"Man, how can you tolerate him? I mean, man, you'd think you'd be on *our* side," he said. "You'd think you'd be with us."

I couldn't help but smile. My partner laughed and the boy clammed up in anger. He slumped back into the seat and stared out the window.

The squad car crawled through the Chicago streets, passing houses asleep in the early dark hours. I looked at the silent windows and the narrow porches and remembered how it was only a few years back.

We lived in a six-room apartment right here on the West Side. Though my mother kept the place clean, the building was shabby and run-down, like those outside the window now.

We were really packed into that apartment on Christiana. Then when I was three years old we moved to another apartment on Springfield Street. There the seven

In this picture taken when I was four years old my grandmother is holding my brand-new cousin Alma. My sister Huchstella is on the left and I am on the right.

of us were once again packed into six rooms — my mother, father, sister, grandmother, two cousins, and I. And, not long after the move, I managed to come down with every childhood disease in the neighborhood. I don't know how my parents managed. But they did. And we were happy.

We lived in the only house in the block with two white posts out front. And there was a backyard where a berry tree grew. I still live with my parents in that apartment on Springfield. It was there that I grew up and made my first contact with gangs, girls, and the guys around the neighborhood.

I remember when we first moved there, my sister, Huchstella, and I would run yelling into the backyard to play. It was the first time we'd had anyplace to play except in front of the house.

"Hey, preacher, how come you so quiet?" the boy in the back seat suddenly said.

His voice brought me back to the real world and away from my childhood. I turned around and looked at him.

At that moment the squad car pulled into the precinct station. My partner turned off the engine and looked across the seat. "Take him in and book him."

"Let's go," I told the boy.

I got out of the car and followed the boy into the

police station. I realized then how lucky I was. Things could have been a lot different. I could have been that boy.

I remembered only too well the things I had done — before I got myself together and straightened out.

Thinking of him I see myself. I couldn't tell the boy, of course, but I had been involved with a street gang like the Vice Lords and the Cobras, and I'd had my share of troubles with the cops. He wasn't much different from what I'd been a few years back.

Then it dawned on me. I had just made my first arrest! I was a police cadet, not a regular officer. Riding in the squad car was just part of my training. I made an arrest and I didn't even have a gun. Man, what if that guy had been armed?

THREE MEALS A DAY

Times haven't changed much. Many kids who grow up in poor neighborhoods are just like me.

I was really brought up by my grandmother, Huchstella Brooks. My mother had to hold down two jobs in order to support the family. She was a schoolteacher and a nurse's aid at night at the hospital.

"Now behave yourself, Bill," I remember my grandmother saying. She spoke in a deep southern accent and, even as a youngster, I remember her talking sometimes about Memphis, Tennessee. "Your mama works hard— and it's all for you. Just remember that."

My mother was our main support for thirteen years. I know she was a good schoolteacher because I was in her class at St. Agatha's. I went there for eight years. Sometimes the only time I saw her was inside the school building.

But I knew how hard she had to work to get us by and I promised myself that someday I'd help out.

My mother isn't very talkative, but she'll go out of her way to help others. She's only five feet five inches tall and weighs 135 pounds — just the opposite of my father, who is a large man — but she has enough energy and willpower for both of them.

"Your father's something of a playboy," she used to tell me. "I knew that when we were married and sometimes I just don't know how I've put up with him."

Then she'd laugh and I knew things were all right.

In the early 1950s, though, things weren't all right and they separated for a while. I'm not sure why they separated, but I can remember hearing voices late in the night.

"Can I help it if I can't get a job?"

My father's voice sounded far away as it came drifting into my brain, which was foggy and cloudy with sleep. "I've looked high and low! I've tried, and it's just no good. Who's going to hire me anyway?"

"Don't talk like that!" My mother was angry. "Why don't you talk to the priest?"

"I ain't talking to no priest."

There was the slam of a door, then silence. Maybe I dreamed it, but I thought I heard weeping.

The next morning the sun came through the window from the backyard. There was nothing on the table, but we didn't say anything.

14

Many mornings were like that. And though my mother worked, we scarcely knew where the next meal was coming from.

Then, one day much later, my father came home. He stood in the doorway grinning, his big frame filling the entire door — at least it looked that way to me, looking up at him.

"I saw the priest," he said. "It took awhile, but I'm working again."

Before he could say anything more, my mother cried out and ran to him, throwing her arms around his neck.

"Hey, let me through!" he said, laughing.

"Where is your job, Daddy?" I asked.

"Hush and let him talk," my sister said. She was a year older than I, and I thought she was kind of bossy.

"Well, I want to know!" I said.

"Be quiet and let your father tell us," my mother said.

"At Hines Hospital," he said.

I could see the pride written all over his face.

"Hines Hospital," he said again. "After six months, I've got a job!"

My mother cried with happiness. I remember her laughing when she went off to work.

"I'll be home at eleven o'clock," she called as she went out the door.

"We'll be here," my father said. A look passed between them and I sensed that his words must have meant more to her than to the rest of us.

I knew that we would no longer have to wait until eleven o'clock at night so she could eat our one meal with us. Now we'd have food three times a day—like other families did.

Things would settle down to normal again.

JUST A DOUGHNUT

"Normal" meant school. My school day started with my mother standing over the bed at six-thirty in the morning shaking my shoulder.

"Bill? William Sims! Wake up!"

I stretched, still half asleep.

"Come on, now. Get dressed. You'll be late."

"I'm coming." I turned over and snuggled deep into the warm cover.

"You going to wear that blanket to school?" my mother asked. She shook me again. "Now get up from there!"

"Yes, ma'am."

I forced myself out of bed. "I'm starved."

My sister was already out of bed and sitting at the table. "You'll get your doughnut when you're dressed," she said when I walked into the kitchen.

"Just a doughnut?" I complained.

"You know you have to go to early Mass and Communion, Bill."

Above, left to right: My sister
Huchstella; a childhood friend, Freddy;
and me at the age of six.

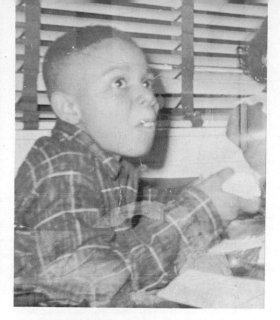

Left: Eating cake at a birthday party for my cousin Alma when I was seven years old.
Below: My sister and I on Easter Sunday when I was six years old.

Left to right: Huchstella, my cousin Susanne, my grandmother, my cousin Alma, and me at the age of eight.

"That don't keep me from being hungry."

"Not don't," she corrected, "doesn't."

"I doesn't like to go hungry," I said, teasing her and letting her know I wasn't really complaining.

"Hurry up and cut out the foolishness," she said, whopping me on the rear end.

"You sure are smart for a seven-year-old," my sister said.

"You're only eight, so shut up!"

"Both of you be quiet." I knew by my mother's voice that she meant business, so I ate my doughnut quietly. When she wasn't looking, I'd make a face at my sister.

By the time we were dressed, Mama had our lunches made. Before I even opened the bag, I knew it was a ham sandwich. Boy, did I get tired of ham sandwiches!

"Behave yourself today," she warned me as I stood on the front steps.

The two white posts in front of the house looked clean in the cold gray morning.

"If I hear of any more trouble, you're going to get it."

"Yes, ma'am," I said.

"He doesn't mean it, Mother," my sister chimed in.

"She's the reason I can't behave," I said to get even.

"Well, you'd better remember what I said," my mother warned again.

21

"Is Father driving us this morning?"

"Not today. You'll have to walk. So go on."

"But school's eleven blocks away," I said.

"Did you know that's more than a mile, Mother?" my sister added.

I made a face at her.

"Show-off!" I shouted.

"Can I help it if I'm smarter than you?"

"Both of you get going before you're late."

My mother hustled us down the steps, and another school day had begun.

MIGHT AS WELL GO HOME

"You going to do it or not?" Larry Simmons asked me. We were standing a block away from my house on the street. There hadn't been anything to do all day and we were bored and restless. Now we'd found something to do, but I wasn't sure if I should get involved or not.

"I don't know," I said.

"You don't know? Man, it'll be a lot of fun, I tell you."

"What happens if we get caught, Larry?"

"Who's going to catch us?" He spit on the sidewalk and squinted up at me.

"The cops, that's who."

"Cops!" Larry said. "They're stupid. What makes you think they'll catch us?"

"I don't know," I said.

I looked down the street. I saw a long line of run-down houses, and shabby wooden and concrete steps. Along the street in front of the houses there was one continuous string of lampposts and streetlights.

23

I looked at the lights glowing and lighting up the street. I looked back at Larry, who was holding a BB gun. He grinned.

"Sure will be fun," he said. Suddenly he just held the gun up and started yelling, "Pop! Pop! Pop-Pop-Pop!" He laughed loudly, then whirled around and put the BB gun to his shoulder. He aimed it toward one of the lights. "That's all there is to it!" he said. "Watch me!"

He ran a few steps away from me and I heard the thud of the BB gun. There was a ting, a sound of glass breaking and suddenly the corner where we stood was a little darker.

That was all I needed.

I laughed with him and shouted, "Let me try it!"

He handed me the BB gun and we ran down the street, shooting out every light we saw. Behind us was a street of darkness. With every broken light we laughed and shouted and jumped in the air.

I had just begun to have fun, to really enjoy myself, when we heard the siren.

"Cops!" Larry yelled. "Get out of here!"

He ran one way and I ran another. We had split up and were halfway home before the policemen could even get out of the car.

I rounded a corner and ducked into an alley.

"Hey! Hey you! Stop! This is the police!"

I couldn't see anyone, but I could tell by the sound of the voice that the policeman was at the other end of the alley. I backed up from the alley and ran down the street.

"Stop! This is the police!"

As I ran, the voice became faint.

I stayed near the house until I thought things had cooled off. Then I went out and tried to find Larry again.

In a little while the City of Chicago or Commonwealth Edison or somebody would be sending out trucks to repair the broken light bulbs. That would give us something to do—stand around and watch the men working high above the street.

I sat on the steps in front of Larry's house. When I saw Larry, he was with another one of my buddies, Willie Harris.

"How you doing, Willie?" I said when he and Larry walked up.

"Okay," he answered.

"You hear anything?" Larry asked me.

"Not yet, but we probably will."

"Larry told me what happened," Willie said. He plopped down on the steps beside me. The street was now so dark that I could barely see him.

"Let's go down and find the others," Larry said.

"Want to go with us, Willie?" I asked.

"Look down there, man," Willie said.

He pointed down the street. All I could see was an endless stretch of dark buildings and shadows.

"If you think I'm walking down there with all the lights out, you're crazy," Willie said.

Suddenly I knew what he meant. Willie was right. If we walked down there now we could get into all kinds of trouble. There had been some rock fights lately between neighborhood gangs and some boys from the next block were out to get even.

They might be waiting for us anywhere down in that dark tunnel of a street and we'd never see them.

I hadn't realized how many lights we had shot out. I had been caught up in the excitement. It seemed to get only a little bit darker each time we hit one.

Now it was dark everywhere and the street was dangerous.

"Hey, Larry," I said. "Now I know why the cops get so angry."

"I just wish they'd hurry up and fix the lights," Larry said. "We might as well go home before it gets any later."

"Yeah," Willie said. "Let's go."

26

MINE'S BROKEN

School was no better. I got into trouble continuously. Some weeks seemed worse than others. Sometimes all I could think was, no stupid schoolteacher is going to tell William Arthur Sims what to do.

I talked in class all the time. I paid no attention to my teachers. When exams came up, Vernon Kuntzman and I would sometimes cheat to pass them.

"Okay, Vernon," I said one day. "Here's what we'll do." We were walking down the hallway of the school. We spoke in low tones. "We've got to get our hands on that test."

Vernon looked at me quickly. "That's crazy," he said.

"You think you can pass it?" I asked.

"Of course not."

"All right, then."

We had come to the end of the hall and two teachers came out of a classroom. They glanced at us, then walked on.

"Look at them," I said. "They got all the answers. Man, they got all the answers."

"What's eating you today?" Vernon asked.

"Nothing," I snapped.

I didn't want to tell him, but I knew I'd never be able to pass the test that was coming up Friday. Rather than study for it, I had been reading comic books.

"We've got to get that test," I told Vernon again.

"How?" he asked.

The two teachers came back through the hall again.

"What are you boys doing?" one of them asked.

"Nothing," I said. "Just talking."

I smiled at them and they went on their way.

"I'll let you know what happens," I told Vernon.

I watched his face closely, searching for some sign that he was impressed by my idea of stealing the test answers. But I saw nothing. Vernon just stared back at me, shook his head, and walked away.

By the time I'd reached my arithmetic class I was feeling sorry for myself and angry.

"Give me your pencil," another boy said to me.

At the sound of the boy's voice I whirled around in my seat and stared at him. "What did you say?" I demanded.

He looked surprised. "All I said, was 'Could I use your pencil for a minute?' Mine's broken."

He held up the yellow pencil and I looked down at the worn tip. The point was no longer sharp, but rounded off into a stub that had cracked. He'd probably studied hard, I told myself.

"Get your own pencil fixed, man!" I hissed at him.

I saw the anger flash across his face, and instantly I was on my feet. My hand sprang out and it caught his shirt front.

He swung at me, and caught me just below the right eye. We went down in a bundle of arms and elbows. We rolled around the floor, bumping desks and cursing each other.

"Cut out that fighting!" somebody yelled.

I couldn't tell if it was the teacher or not. I was halfway under a desk, the boy still pounding my face. "Break it up!"

"Hit him again, Roy!" somebody yelled.

"Yeah, Roy! He started it! Get him Roy!"

I lashed out, striking him on the chest. I managed to get him off me, but by the time I could stand up the classroom teacher had him by the collar with one hand, and me with the other.

"Break it up!" the teacher shouted. "I'm ashamed of both of you! Good Catholic boys fighting like this!"

"He started it!" Roy said.

"Is that right, Bill?" The teacher looked at me. I was silent for a moment, then I nodded my head.

"All right," the teacher said. She released Roy and told him to go clean himself up in the bathroom.

"You come with me," she said.

She walked in front of me. I followed along behind with my head hanging. When I passed her desk I saw the test answers. They were just lying there as if they were waiting for me. Quickly, I snatched the sheet of paper and stuffed it into my shirt. Nobody saw me. I followed the teacher to the door. She stopped and waited for me.

"See those steps, young man?" she asked.

"Yes."

"Well, you'll spend your lunch hours there from now on. Do you understand?"

When she turned and walked back to the class, I smiled to myself.

My hand reached inside my shirt and I felt the paper crinkled there.

GOOD OLD ERNIE

My mother was a schoolteacher, and she demanded good grades. You can't steal every test, so most of the time I had to study.

When I graduated from grade school I started at Quigley Seminary, a Catholic high school on the South Side.

One of my best friends from high school was Stanley Turner. Stanley and I teamed up to become the two damndest liars anyone ever heard of.

We took the bus to school in the morning.

"We're late again, Stanley. What are we going to tell them this time?"

"Well, we were walking down the street on our way to school, see . . ."

"Yeah."

". . . and this old lady stopped us and asked us if we'd help her look for her dog."

"We couldn't turn down a request from an old lady," I said.

This picture was taken in June of 1962 at
my eighth grade graduation from St. Agatha's.

"Certainly not, especially since the poor old thing was crippled and half blind."

"How could a poor blind lady find her dog all by herself?"

"That's right. Now you're getting it, and the dog was a huge Doberman pinscher."

"Man, did that dog give us a hell of a chase."

Somehow, Stanley and I managed to pull these fantastic stories off. I don't know how we did it.

There were gangs in the neighborhood. The big ones were the Vice Lords and the Cobras. I knew just about every member of these gangs, and at one time I was a member of both of them at the same time. Both gangs trusted me, and at times I served as a mediator between them.

The gangs were almost always on the brink of war. There were times when one gang member could not cross the street into another gang's territory. I could cross the street, and I often brought messages from one gang to another. More than once I helped prevent a gang war. I was lucky enough to be able to stay away from the gang's other activities — burglary, robbery, shoplifting, and a host of others.

When I was sixteen, Stanley Turner and I told the ultimate lie.

"Sure we know Ernie Banks," Stanley told Andy. "Don't we, Bill?"

"You better believe we do. Hell, we had dinner over at Ernie's place just last Saturday."

Andy was tough to convince.

"Oh, man, everyone knows that you two guys are the biggest bull artists in the neighborhood."

"All right, don't believe us then, but Ernie gave us a couple of tickets to the doubleheader Sunday. Nice guy, that Ernie. Box seats, too."

One day just after the baseball season ended Andy ran up to us.

"I been looking for you guys all over the place. Guess who's standing in front of the YMCA talking to people?"

"Who's that?"

"Ernie Banks, that's who. Your old buddy."

Oh, no! Not Banks himself.

"And the three of us are going over there to meet your buddy. Come on! Let's go! I been listening to your talk long enough."

We couldn't back down now. We had already gone too far. We walked with Andy toward the YMCA. When we got there a crowd of people surrounded Ernie Banks.

We started pushing toward the front. Stanley and I got ahead of Andy.

Stanley whispered to me, "Try to hold Andy back a little. I'm going to try something."

I walked slow.

"Come on, let's go," Andy said, pushing at me.

"Don't worry, we'll get there."

When Stanley got to the front of the crowd I heard him shout, "Ernie, how's it going, kid?"

I pushed my way to the front. Banks looked confused while Stanley stood pumping his hand like an old friend. Then Stanley put his head close to Banks' ear.

"Please, Mr. Banks," he whispered. "We told everyone in the neighborhood that we were good friends of yours."

"Do you know these guys, Mr. Banks?" Andy shouted from behind us.

"Please," Stanley whispered again.

"Why . . . why sure, sure. How's it going, boys?"

I sighed with relief.

"How are you today, er . . ." Banks fumbled.

"Stanley," Stanley whispered.

"Bill," I added.

"Sure, Stanley and Bill. I haven't seen you boys for a long time. What you been up to?"

"I'll be damned. I'll be damned," Andy said.

Good old Ernie. He really is a nice guy.

CHANGING THINGS

When I opened my eyes and stared around the room the first thing I heard was my sister and mother moving around in the other room, already starting to clean.

Saturday always began with work, so I hopped out of bed, and pulled on my trousers. My job at home was to gather all the clothes that needed washing or cleaning. I scurried around, hurrying, so I would be finished by noon.

What would I do today, I wondered?

Of course I'd have to go down and see what the kids were up to.

Maybe, I thought, the school had planned a field trip down to the museum and they'd forgotten to tell me about it. Boy, that would be a pleasant surprise, I told myself.

I pulled a batch of clothes from the closet and dumped them into a sheet. I gathered in the four ends of the sheet, pulled them together, and managed to tie a knot. The clothes now were all bundled up.

No, if there was a museum trip, I'd know about it. I still didn't know what I'd do when I finished working at home.

At that moment the telephone rang. I dropped the bundle of clothes and ran through the house yelling, "I'll get it! I'll get it!" I beat my sister to the telephone.

"Hello?"

It was my uncle.

"Have you finished your work?" he asked.

"Just about. I've only got a little more to do."

"Well, listen," he said. "Hurry up and finish. I'll be over around noon. I thought the two of us could drive up to Wisconsin for a while."

"Yes, sir!" I shouted. "I'll finish right away!"

"Who was it?" my sister asked.

"Who else but my dear, sweet, loving uncle who's going to take me to Wisconsin."

"Oh," my sister said. She flitted out of the room dismissing me and my uncle and the trip. She had other things to do that were more important, she told me.

I worked hard and fast all Saturday morning and when my uncle's car pulled up in front of the house, I was ready.

I ran out, hopped into the front seat, and soon we were on our way. We passed through Chicago, then out onto the expressway toward Wisconsin.

At the age of sixteen in my parents' home.

I was happy because I knew in a little while we'd be fishing on some quiet riverbank.

"Here we are," he said after awhile.

The two of us climbed out of the car, got our fishing gear together, and walked into the cool, silent forest. The trees were tall and sunlight filtered down in bright circles on the pine needles. The woods smelled wintergreen fresh and after we had walked a little while we could smell the water.

"Sure is a nice day," my uncle said. "I hope we catch some big ones."

We worked our way through the woods and came out on the riverbank. In front of me the water flowed smooth ly, and out toward the middle, I could see tiny ripples catching the sunlight and bouncing it back like a million tiny mirrors.

We sat on the bank, threw the lines into the water, and sat waiting for the first bite. We waited in silence for an hour without a nibble. Suddenly my uncle turned and looked at me.

"Bill," he said, "you'll be finishing high school soon, what are you going to do?"

"I don't know," I told him. Our voices were the only sounds, drifting across the water. The fish were not biting so we were not disturbed.

"You seem to be down in the dumps lately," my uncle said. "Something bothering you?"

"Maybe you just named it. I don't know what I'm going to do."

"You'll always have to work hard.

"I expect that. But I don't want to spend the rest of my spare time hanging around street corners."

He smiled at me, threw his line farther out into the water, and said, "There's somebody I want you to meet sometime."

"Who?" I asked.

"Fellow I know who heads the Neighborhood Youth Corps."

"Oh," I said, disappointed. It didn't sound like what I had in mind.

But, while sitting there on the riverbank fishing, I made up my mind to go ahead and meet this guy, just for my uncle's sake. After all, he'd done me a lot of favors, taking me fishing and letting me talk.

That was the beginning of my first job. That summer, to keep from just hanging around the streets, I started working with the Neighborhood Youth Corps.

Some of our projects included repainting and cleaning up the elementary school. It was fun slapping new paint on the old walls.

During my junior year of high school on a trip to Springfield, Illinois. My friend John Calicott is sitting next to the window of the train.

When we finished that project that summer, I stood looking at the gleaming bright elementary school. Suddenly I was very happy. I had helped turn the dilapidated building into something fresh and new and fun for children to be in.

The feeling was a good one. I still didn't know what I wanted to do with my life, but I had started changing things.

I even took a new interest in my schoolwork when classes started in the fall. I studied hard and made good grades until my graduation in June.

DECISIONS

Should I go to college? Why not? I had quit stealing tests, and had started studying in high school. I had become a good student.

I enrolled in Loyola University, which pleased my mother and father tremendously.

There I majored in psychology. I was fascinated by this field because I wanted to learn why people act as they do. If I could find out some of these things, I felt I could understand myself better.

But I needed money to go to college and I knew that I'd have to work. My mother and father would never have been able to send me with their income alone and though the Neighborhood Youth Corps was fun, it didn't provide an income.

So I started looking around for a job.

I wasn't having much luck, but one day the postman left a form in our mailbox. It said that the post office was looking for qualified employees.

"Why don't you try it?" my mother asked.

I went through the usual procedures of filling out forms and answering questions, and when it was all over I suddenly found myself an employee of the United States Post Office.

Now it seemed as if the days would never end. I worked eight hours a day at the post office, and jumped on the bus for Loyola for two or three hours of classes each night.

Then I rode home, studying on the bus. I had to stay up late and squeeze study hours in anyplace I could — lunchtime at the post office, at the breakfast table, riding the buses, anywhere.

I made a friend at the post office, a white kid named Art. He was in the same bag I was, working at the post office full time, and going to Loyola at night. We often rode the bus together.

"Damn, I hate to go to school feeling so crumby," I said. "We get no chance to take a shower. No chance to do anything. Just change clothes and take off."

"Yeah, I know," Art said. "We throw mail sacks around all day, and then rush to school at night. Hell, last night my armpits stank so bad I was afraid to raise my hand in class."

I laughed. "You mean if you raised your hand the girl next to you would faint. Is that it?"

"Yeah, that's it."

When I was in my third year at Loyola I met an old buddy of mine from the neighborhood, "Curly" Russell. We called him Curly because he was completely bald.

"What are you doing these days, Curly?" I asked.

"You wouldn't believe me if I told you, man. I'm a police cadet."

"You? A cop?"

"Not a cop. Not yet, anyway. I'm a cadet. I won't be a cop until I complete my training a year from now."

I was shocked.

"You're going to be a cop," I said shaking my head. "And I remember all the things you used to do on these streets."

"I don't have a record."

"That's only because you never got caught," I laughed.

"Why don't you think about it, Bill? You've never been in any trouble, have you?"

"No. I don't have any kind of record either."

"I'll tell you, man, for an interesting job you can't beat it. Let me tell you what happened last night . . ."

Curly and I spent the afternoon together. He convinced me. I wanted to become a police cadet.

I took the tests and passed all the requirements. In May, 1969, I became a Chicago police cadet.

APPETITE FOR ACTION

I imagined myself as a policeman and the thoughts were pleasant. I felt that I would be responsible for people — for their safety and for helping them when they got into trouble.

And I would see a lot of action. I would be in on everything that happened in the city. I hoped all my old contacts with the gangs would help me understand people better.

I knew that I was beginning a career. I would become something in life after all.

"All right, Sims," they told me during the first week. "You can forget all this nonsense about going out and arresting people."

"But I thought . . ."

"Let me finish," the Captain said. "You'll get involved in the action one of these days, but not until you understand the department thoroughly. You have to learn how to operate and why we do the things we do.

"Yes, sir," I said, feeling a bit disappointed.

"Don't look so grim," the Captain said. "You've got to learn to walk before you can run, and the best way I know how to teach you is to start at the communications desk."

I was worried that I'd be bored working the phones at night. I found I was wrong. I worked in the Fillmore District. The toughest section of the city.

A call came in.

"There's a man outside with a knife."

"What's the address, sir?" I asked.

"He's just standing in the middle of the street with this big knife. He must be nuts or something. You guys better pick him up. He's got to be nuts."

"What's the address, sir?" I asked again, louder this time.

"He's on the corner of Madison and Sacramento. He's standing in the middle of Madison with his big knife . . ."

I turned to the radio to dispatch a squad car.

"Madison and Sacramento, man with a knife."

Some of the calls sounded serious at first, but turned out to be nothing.

"My husband is trying to kill me!" A woman screamed into the phone.

"Where do you live, lady?" I asked.

"What difference does that make?"

47

"Well, lady, how can we help you out if we don't know where you live?"

"Are you getting fresh with me, officer?"

I tried to stay calm.

"No, lady. I'm trying to help you. Now if you'll just tell me where you live I'll send a squad over there."

"I think you want to pick me up. That's what you want to do."

"Where is your husband now, ma'am?"

"He died three years ago."

"He's dead, but he's still trying to kill you?"

"Yes. And all you want is my address. Why, we don't even know each other. I should have known better than to call the police. All you police are fresh, and . . ."

Behind the main desk at Fillmore Station,
where I was assigned as a police cadet.

49

OFFICER SIMS

I walked out of the Eleventh District station where I'd just booked the young boy for breaking and entering. As I came down the front steps my partner still waited in the squad car.

"What in the world are you thinking about?" he asked, when I crawled into the front seat.

"About everything," I told him. "About how I started out and how I could have been just like that boy and how I wound up instead being a cop."

My partner laughed.

"That's because you're smarter than he is," he said.

"Not really. I was just luckier and I found what I wanted to do with my life. Maybe he will, too, someday."

"And the communications unit didn't tear down any of your enthusiasm?" my partner asked.

"God, no," I said. "As a matter of fact it just whetted my appetite for action. I'm glad I've finally been transferred, though. I couldn't take that desk job much longer."

The hat I wear as a police cadet does not have the
checkerboard squares of a full-fledged policeman's uniform.

He laughed, put the car in gear, and we moved out into the night streets.

"By the way, I'd have felt a little safer if I'd had a gun," I said.

"I know what you mean, Sims."

I reached down, unfastened the gun belt and placed it on the seat between us.

"Just remember you're still only twenty years old, William Arthur Sims."

"All right, all right!"

"And twenty-year-old policemen are not allowed to carry side arms."

"I know all that," I said, still laughing.

"You'll have a gun when you turn just another year older."

"Then I'll be a full-fledged police officer," I said softly.

I couldn't help it, but the pride swelled within me and I felt the same joy I had felt that first moment when I put on the uniform.

It was going to be a good life, after all, I decided. A darn good life.

The squad car eased through the streets quietly and we waited calmly for the next radio call.

Patrolman Richard Iwanowski is showing me the standard police shotgun.

52

Not all police work is exciting — there is
much routine paperwork, including typing and filing.

In the Youth Division office at Fillmore
Station; Youth Officer Madkin is on the left.

CAREER GUIDANCE

POLICEMEN AND POLICEWOMEN*

Nature of Work

Police officers — whether directing traffic at busy intersections or arresting dangerous criminals — are helping to preserve law and order. As local government employees, their job is to prevent criminal activities, to investigate crimes, and to apprehend and assist in the prosecution of offenders. Whether on duty or off duty, they are expected to exercise their authority whenever necessary.

The policeman who works in a small community customarily handles many kinds of police duties. He may, for example, direct traffic at the scene of a fire, investigate a housebreaking, and give first aid to an accident victim — all in the course of a day's work.

In a large police department, officers are usually assigned to a specific type of police duty. Most policemen are detailed either to patrol or traffic duty; smaller numbers are assigned to

*Career information adapted from the United States Department of Labor Occupational Outlook Handbook.

special work, such as accident prevention or operating radio and other communications systems. Some officers are detectives (plainclothesmen) assigned to criminal investigation, and others are experts in chemical and microscopic analysis, firearms identification, and other investigative specialties. In very large cities, a few officers may be specially trained for work with mounted and motorcycle police, harbor patrols, helicopter patrols, canine corps, or mobile rescue teams.

An increasing number of city police departments are including women on their police forces. Policewomen are usually assigned to work which involves women and young people. They may, for example, work with juvenile delinquents, try to locate lost children and runaways, or search, question, book, and fingerprint women prisoners. Less frequently, they are assigned to detective squads, where they work mainly on crimes involving women.

Most newly recruited policemen begin on patrol duty. Patrolmen may be assigned to congested business districts, outlying residential areas, or other sections of a city; they may cover their beats alone or with other patrolmen; and they may ride in a police vehicle or walk on "foot" patrol. In any case, they become thoroughly familiar with conditions throughout their area and while on patrol, remain alert for anything out of the ordinary. They note suspicious circumstances, such as open windows or lights in vacant buildings, as well as hazards to public safety, such as burned-out streetlights or fallen trees. Patrolmen also may watch for stolen automobiles and enforce traffic regulations. They report to police headquarters at regular intervals through call boxes or by radio, giving and receiving information about any situations which require action. They also prepare and turn in reports about their activities and, in cases which result in legal action, they may be called upon to give testimony in court.

Where Employed

An estimated 275,000 full-time policemen and policewomen were employed in 1967 by local government police departments. Some cities — including New York City with almost 28,000 police officers, and Chicago with over 10,000 — have very large police forces, while hundreds of small cities employ fewer than 25 policemen each. Policewomen work mainly in large cities.

Training, Other Qualifications, and Advancement

Local civil service regulations govern the appointment of police officers in practically all large cities and in many small ones. Candidates must be United States citizens, usually at least twenty-one years of age, and be able to meet certain height and weight standards.

Eligibility for appointment is also determined by the candidates' performance on competitive examinations, their physical and personal qualifications, and their education and experience. The physical examinations often include tests of strength and agility. Also, because personal characteristics such as honesty, good judgment, and a sense of responsibility are especially important in police work, candidates are usually interviewed by a senior officer at police headquarters, and their character traits and background also may be investigated.

Some police departments accept men with less than a high school education as recruits, particularly if they have had work experience in a field related to law enforcement. In large police departments, where most jobs are to be found, applicants must usually have at least a high school education. A few cities require some college training, and some hire law enforcement students as police interns.

Police departments are placing increasing emphasis on post-high school training in subjects such as sociology, psychology, and minority group relations with the result that more than one hundred colleges and universities now offer major programs in law enforcement. Physical education and sports activities are especially helpful to men in developing the physical stamina and agility needed in police work. College training is likely to be required for policewomen, because of their specialized assignments. Training or experience in social work, teaching, or nursing is considered desirable.

Young men who have completed high school and do not want to wait until they are twenty-one years old before entering police work can start in some very large cities by working as police cadets, or trainees, while still in their teens. As paid civilian employees of the police department, they attend classes part of the time to learn various aspects of police science, and also do clerical and other nonenforcement work. When police cadets or trainees reach the age of twenty-one—and provided they qualify in other respects—they may be appointed to the police force.

Before being sent out on their first assignments, policemen usually go through a period of training. The instruction is given informally in many small communities, as recruits work for a week or so with experienced officers.

More extensive training, such as that provided in large city police departments, may extend over a period of several weeks or a few months and includes classroom instruction in constitutional law and civil rights, as well as in state laws and local ordinances, and in the procedures to be followed in accident investigation, patrol, traffic control, and other police work. Recruits learn how to use a gun, defend themselves from attack, administer first aid, and deal with other emergencies.

Policemen and policewomen generally become eligible for

promotion after completing specified periods of service on the force; and in a large department, this may open the way for an officer to specialize in one of several kinds of law enforcement activities—laboratory work, traffic control, communications, work with juveniles, and many others. Promotions are made in accordance with each candidate's position on a promotion list, as determined by his performance on written examinations and his work as a police officer. Opportunities to advance are generally most numerous in large police departments, where the work is carried on in separate bureaus under the direction of administrative officers and their assistants. Most top ranking positions are occupied by men. Opportunities for women to advance beyond the rank of sergeant are mainly in the few police departments which have separate bureaus for women and juveniles.

Many types of training are available to help police officers improve their performance on the job and prepare themselves for advancement. Through training given at police department academies and at colleges and other institutions, officers have opportunities to become informed or keep abreast of such varied subjects as crowd control techniques, civil defense, legal developments which affect policemen, the interrogation of suspects and witnesses, and the advances in electronic and other types of equipment being developed as an aid to law enforcement. Many police departments encourage officers to work toward college degrees, and some pay all or part of the tuition

Employment Outlook

During the rest of the 1960s and through the 1970s, an estimated 15,000 opportunities will occur each year for qualified candidates to enter police work. Thousands will be new positions which arise as cities increase the size of their police forces to meet the needs of a growing population. Most openings, however, will be vacancies that occur as policemen and policewomen retire or leave their jobs for other reasons. Police officers usually retire at a somewhat younger age than workers in most other occupations, and replacement rates are relatively high for this reason.

Police employment is expected to rise moderately during the next ten years, as population and economic growth create a need for more officers to protect life and property, regulate traffic, and provide other police services.

The kinds of police jobs that arise in the future are likely to be affected to a considerable degree by changes now taking place in police methods and equipment. Specialists are becoming more and more essential in the effective operation of modern city police departments. In an increasing number of departments, for example, electronic data processing is being used to compile administrative, criminal, and identification records. There is a greater need also for officers with specialized training, as engineering techniques are applied to traffic planning and control and social work techniques are used in crime prevention. At the same time, relatively fewer officers are required for routine assignments, such as directing traffic, because of the use of automatic signal lights to control traffic at busy intersections.

Although the vast majority of new jobs that arise will be for men, many openings will occur for women also.

Earnings and Working Conditions

In 1966, entrance salaries for police officers ranged from

less than $3,000 a year in some small cities to almost $7,500 in several large ones.

Most policemen and policewomen receive regular pay increases during the first few years of employment, until a specified maximum is reached. Sergeants, lieutenants, and captains are paid progressively higher basic salaries than patrolmen in the same police departments. Top salaries are paid to police chiefs or commissioners, and in 1966 their salaries ranged from less than $5,000 a year in some small cities to more than $35,000 in the largest cities.

Police departments usually provide officers with special allowances for uniforms, and furnish revolvers, nightsticks, handcuffs, and other equipment required.

The scheduled workweek for police officers is usually forty hours, and in localities where the workweek is longer — weekly hours are being gradually reduced. Police protection must be provided round the clock, and in all but the very smallest communities, some officers are usually on duty over weekends, on holidays, and at night. Policemen are subject to call at any time their services may be needed and, in emergencies, may work overtime. Overtime, in some departments, is paid at straight time or time and a half; in others, officers may be given an equal amount of time off on another day of the week.

Police officers are generally covered by liberal pension plans, under which many are able to retire at half pay by the time they reach fifty-five. Paid vacations, sick leave, and medical, surgical, and life insurance plans are among the other benefits frequently provided.

Policemen may be assigned to work outdoors for long periods in all kinds of weather. The injury rate is higher than in many occupations and reflects the risks police officers take in pursuing speeding motorists, capturing lawbreakers, and dealing with disorderly conduct cases.

Where To Go for More Information

Information about local entrance requirements may be obtained from local civil service commissions or police departments.

Additional information on the occupations of policemen and policewomen may be obtained from:

International Association of Chiefs of Police
1319 18th St. N.W., Washington, D.C. 20036

International Association of Women Police
100 North La Salle St.
Chicago, Illinois 60602

Additional information on the salaries and hours of work of policemen in various cities is published by The International City Managers' Association in its *Municipal Yearbook*, available in many libraries.